Inspiration

GARDEN

VERSE

Time, Love & Beauty

Publisher and Creative Director: Nick Wells
Commissioning Editor: Polly Prior
Editorial Assistant: Taylor Bentley
Art Director and Layout Design: Mike Spender
Digital Design and Production: Chris Herbert

FLAME TREE PUBLISHING

6 Melbray Mews
London SW6 3NS
United Kingdom

www.flametreepublishing.com
First published 2019

19 21 23 22 20
1 3 5 7 9 10 8 6 4 2

Every effort has been made to contact copyright holders. In the event of an oversight the publishers would be glad to rectify any omissions in future editions of this book.

A CIP record for this book is available from the British Library upon request.

ISBN 978-1-78755-278-4

Printed in China | Created, Developed & Produced in the United Kingdom

Inspiration

GARDEN

VERSE

Time, Love & Beauty

Introduction by
Rachael Allen

FLAME TREE
PUBLISHING

CONTENTS

INTRODUCTION

Alice Oswald, the contemporary British poet known for her knowledge of classics, gardening, ecology and landscape, said that 'what's important is that listening, and gardening as a form of listening, is a way of forcing a poem open to what lies bodily beyond it.' When we sit, work, or relax in the garden, we are gifted a space outside of the confines of a bricks-and-mortar home. We see and hear things differently, we are able to commune with a cultivated ecological space.

In Amy Lowell's lush and replete poem 'Behind A Wall', she too talks of the listening space of a garden:

> *So far and still it is that, listening,*
> *I hear the flowers taking in the dawn*

The space of a garden feels inherently bound to the space of a poem in this way, as both poems and gardens instil in the reader and the garden dweller the importance of sound, of listening, and then of being open to lives that exist outside of our own subjectivities. And poems are best when they open us up to experiences outside of ourselves, while retaining an emotional thread to something familiar in the human experience. A garden is this, a cultivated but wild space that is both familiar to us, that will always exist outside of us, however much we prune and tend. We can curate it as much as we like, but it will always grow away from us, to its own dictate. And there can be a darkness in this unfamiliarity. If we consider William Blake's 'The Sick Rose', in which 'worms', 'roses' and 'wind' become spectres within his poem-long metaphor, the constructed binary between what is human and what is 'natural' are brought together with a material force. Roses, a plant bred and cultivated out by human hands, is considered alongside the bodily anomaly of disease.

Poems often chart changes in our lives, similarly to how we can chart changes by watching our gardens move and grow. In Charlotte Mew's 'The Trees are Down', she empathises with the plane-trees as they are cut down at the end of her garden. This nudges her thinking towards seasonal and emotional changes, and thoughts on the passing of life. She aligns her own life with the trees, having lived with them 'in the sun, in the rains', a commingling of human body and plant life, a metaphor on what sustains us, the inescapability of the passage of time. Similarly, in Walt Whitman's 'This Compost', life is charted through what is found living and growing on the earth, and what is rotting beneath: 'The bean bursts noiselessly through the mould in the garden', 'the delicate spear of the onion pierces upward', 'The new-born of animals appear', to which he concludes, 'What chemistry!' It could be that he is talking both of the cyclical chemistry of what it means to exist on earth, the inherent chemistry in a poem, and the various and multiple chemistries that exists outside of us, in our gardens, the things that gift us 'such divine materials'.

Poems and gardens are wed in these ways – a reminder of an ecological existence that precedes us, that we depend on, and that is wedded to our human history. The best of the poems about gardens, and the best of poems in general, remind us of this fact. Like gardens, they are a small space for us to listen and practice the work of being receptive, to contemplate and to consider.

Rachael Allen

Paradise Lost
And Found

Spirituality and Religion

Flower in the Crannied Wall

Flower in the crannied wall,
I pluck you out of the crannies,
I hold you here, root and all, in my hand,
Little flower – but *if* I could understand
What you are, root and all, all in all,
I should know what God and man is.

Alfred, Lord Tennyson (1809-1892)

The Garden

How vainly men themselves amaze
To win the palm, the oak, or bays;
And their uncessant labors see
Crowned from some single herb or tree,
Whose short and narrow-vergèd shade
Does prudently their toils upbraid;
While all the flowers and trees do close
To weave the garlands of repose.

Fair Quiet, have I found thee here,
And Innocence, thy sister dear!
Mistaken long, I sought you then
In busy companies of men:
Your sacred plants, if here below,
Only among the plants will grow;
Society is all but rude,
To this delicious solitude.

No white nor red was ever seen
So amorous as this lovely green;
Fond lovers, cruel as their flame,

Cut in these trees their mistress' name.
Little, alas, they know or heed,
How far these beauties hers exceed!
Fair trees! wheresoe'er your barks I wound
No name shall but your own be found.

When we have run our passion's heat,
Love hither makes his best retreat:
The gods who mortal beauty chase,
Still in a tree did end their race.
Apollo hunted Daphne so,
Only that she might laurel grow,
And Pan did after Syrinx speed,
Not as a nymph, but for a reed.

What wondrous life is this I lead!
Ripe apples drop about my head;
The luscious clusters of the vine
Upon my mouth do crush their wine;
The nectarine and curious peach
Into my hands themselves do reach;
Stumbling on melons as I pass,
Insnared with flowers, I fall on grass.

Meanwhile the mind, from pleasure less,
Withdraws into its happiness:
The mind, that ocean where each kind
Does straight its own resemblance find;
Yet it creates, transcending these,
Far other worlds, and other seas;
Annihilating all that's made
To a green thought in a green shade.

Here at the fountain's sliding foot,
Or at some fruit-tree's mossy root,
Casting the body's vest aside,
My soul into the boughs does glide:
There like a bird it sits and sings,
Then whets and combs its silver wings;
And, till prepared for longer flight,
Waves in its plumes the various light.

Such was that happy garden-state,
While man there walked without a mate:
After a place so pure and sweet,
What other help could yet be meet!
But 'twas beyond a mortal's share

To wander solitary there:
Two paradises 'twere in one
To live in Paradise alone.

How well the skillful gard'ner drew
Of flowers and herbs this dial new;
Where from above the milder sun
Does through a fragrant zodiac run;
And, as it works, th' industrious bee
Computes its time as well as we.
How could such sweet and wholesome hours
Be reckoned but with herbs and flowers!

Andrew Marvell (1621-1678)

A Garden Song

Here, in this sequestered close
Bloom the hyacinth and rose;
Here beside the modest stock
Flaunts the flaring hollyhock;
Here, without a pang, one sees
Ranks, conditions, and degrees.

All the seasons run their race
In this quiet resting place;
Peach, and apricot, and fig
Here will ripen, and grow big;
Here is store and overplus, –
More had not Alcinoüs!

Here, in alleys cool and green,
Far ahead the thrush is seen;
Here along the southern wall
Keeps the bee his festival;
All is quiet else – afar
Sounds of toil and turmoil are.

Here be shadows large and long;
Here be spaces meet for song;
Grant, O garden-god, that I,
Now that none profane is nigh, –
Now that mood and moment please,
Find the fair Pierides!

Austin Dobson (1840-1921)

SHUT OUT

The door was shut. I looked between
Its iron bars; and saw it lie,
My garden, mine, beneath the sky,
Pied with all flowers bedewed and green:

From bough to bough the song-birds crossed,
From flower to flower the moths and bees;
With all its nests and stately trees
It had been mine, and it was lost.

A shadowless spirit kept the gate,
Blank and unchanging like the grave.
I peering through said: 'Let me have
Some buds to cheer my outcast state.'

He answered not. 'Or give me, then,
But one small twig from shrub or tree;
And bid my home remember me
Until I come to it again.'

The spirit was silent; but he took
Mortar and stone to build a wall;
He left no loophole great or small
Through which my straining eyes might look:

So now I sit here quite alone
Blinded with tears; nor grieve for that,
For nought is left worth looking at
Since my delightful land is gone.

A violet bed is budding near,
Wherein a lark has made her nest:
And good they are, but not the best;
And dear they are, but not so dear.

Christina Rossetti (1830-1894)

EVE

Close to the gates of Paradise I flee;
The night is hot and serpents leave their beds,
And slide along the dark, crooking their heads, –
My God, my God, open the gates to me!

My eyes are burning so I cannot see;
My feet are bleeding and I suffer pain;
Let me come in on the cool grass again –
My God, my God, open the gates to me!

I ate the fruit of the forbidden tree,
And was cast out into the barren drouth;
And since – the awful taste within my mouth!
My God, my God, open the gates to me!

Am I shut out for all eternity?
I do repent me of my one black sin,
With prayers and tears of blood . . . Let me come in!
My God, my God, open the gates to me!

Let me come in where birds and flowers be;
Let me once more lie naked in the grass
That trembles when the long wind-ripples pass!
Lord God, Lord God, open the gates to me!

Ella Higginson (1861-1940)

Four-Leaf Clover

I know a place where the sun is like gold,
And the cherry blooms burst with snow,
And down underneath is the loveliest nook,
Where the four-leaf clovers grow.

One leaf is for hope, and one is for faith,
And one is for love, you know,
And God put another in for luck –
If you search, you will find where they grow.

But you must have hope, and you must have faith,
You must love and be strong – and so –
If you work, if you wait, you will find the place
Where the four-leaf clovers grow.

Ella Higginson (1861-1940)

EUTOPIA

There is a garden where lilies
And roses are side by side;
And all day between them in silence
The silken butterflies glide.

I may not enter the garden,
Though I know the road thereto;
And morn by morn to the gateway
I see the children go.

They bring back light on their faces;
But they cannot bring back to me
What the lilies say to the roses,
Or the songs of the butterflies be.

Francis Turner Palgrave (1824-1897)

The Horticulturists's Table-Hymn

From him, who was lord of the fruits and the flowers,
That in Paradise grew, ere he lost its possession –
Who breathed in the balm, and reposed in the bowers
Of our garden ancestral, we claim our profession.
And fruits rich and bright
Bless our taste and our sight
As e'er gave our father in Eden delight:
Our fount clear as that, which he drank from, here flows;
Where green grows the myrtle, and blushing the rose.

While some sit in clouds but to murmur, or grieve
That earth has her wormwood, her pitfalls, and brambles;
We smile, and go forth her rich gifts to receive,
Where the boughs drop their purple and gold on
    our rambles.
Untiring and free,
As we work, like the bee,
We bear off a sweet from each plant, shrub, and tree:
Where some gather thorns but to torture the flesh,
Ripe clusters we pluck, and our spirits refresh.

Yet, not to self only, we draw from the soil
The treasures that Heaven in its vitals hath hidden;
For thus to lock up the fair fruits of our toil
Were bliss half possessed, and a sin all forbidden.
Like morning's first ray,
When it spreads into day,
Our hearts must flow out, until self melts away!
Our joys, in the bosoms around us when sown,
Spring up and bloom out, throwing sweets to our own.

And this makes the world all a garden to us,
Where He, who has walled it, his glory is shedding:
His smile is its sun; and beholding it thus,
We gratefully feast, while his bounty is spreading.
Our spirits grow bright
As they bathe in his light,
That beams on the board where in joy we unite:
And the sparks, which we take to enkindle our mirth,
Are blessings from heaven showering down on the earth.
And now that we meet, and the chain is of *flowers*,

Which binds us together, may sadness ne'er blight them,

Till those, who *must* break from a compact like ours,

Ascend where the ties of the blest reunite them!

May each, who is here,

At the banquet appear,

Where Life fills the wine-cup, and Love makes it clear;

And Gilead's balm in its freshness shall flow

On the wounds, which the *pruning-knife* gave us below!

Hannah F. Gould (1789-1865)

The Summer Bower

It is a place whither I've often gone
For peace, and found it, secret, hushed, and cool,
A beautiful recess in neighboring woods.
Trees of the soberest hues, thick-leaved and tall,
Arch it o'erhead and column it around,
Framing a covert, natural and wild,
Domelike and dim; though nowhere so enclosed
But that the gentlest breezes reach the spot
Unwearied and unweakened. Sound is here
A transient and unfrequent visitor;
Yet if the day be calm, not often then,
Whilst the high pines in one another's arms
Sleep, you may sometimes with unstartled ear
Catch the far fall of voices, how remote
You know not, and you do not care to know.
The turf is soft and green, but not a flower
Lights the recess, save one, star-shaped and bright –
I do not know its name – which here and there
Gleams like a sapphire set in emerald.
A narrow opening in the branchëd roof,
A single one, is large enough to show,

With that half glimpse a dreamer loves so much,

The blue air and the blessing of the sky.

Thither I always bent my idle steps,

When griefs depressed, or joys disturbed my heart,

And found the calm I looked for, or returned

Strong with the quiet rapture in my soul.

But one day,

One of those July days when winds have fled

One knows not whither, I, most sick in mind

With thoughts that shall be nameless, yet, no doubt,

Wrong, or at least unhealthful, since though dark

With gloom, and touched with discontent, they had

No adequate excuse, nor cause, nor end,

I, with these thoughts, and on this summer day,

Entered the accustomed haunt, and found for once

No medicinal virtue.

Not a leaf

Stirred with the whispering welcome which I sought,

But in a close and humid atmosphere,

Every fair plant and implicated bough

Hung lax and lifeless. Something in the place,

Its utter stillness, the unusual heat,

And some more secret influence, I thought,
Weighed on the sense like sin. Above I saw,
Though not a cloud was visible in heaven,
The pallid sky look through a glazèd mist
Like a blue eye in death.
                            The change, perhaps,
Was natural enough; my jaundiced sight,
The weather, and the time explain it all:
Yet have I drawn a lesson from the spot,
And shrined it in these verses for my heart.
Thenceforth those tranquil precincts I have sought
Not less, and in all shades of various moods;
But always shun to desecrate the spot
By vain repinings, sickly sentiments,
Or inconclusive sorrows. Nature, though
Pure as she was in Eden when her breath
Kissed the white brow of Eve, doth not refuse,
In her own way and with a just reserve,
To sympathize with human suffering;
But for the pains, the fever, and the fret
Engendered of a weak, unquiet heart,
She hath no solace; and who seeks her when

These be the troubles over which he moans,

Reads in her unreplying lineaments

Rebukes, that, to the guilty consciousness,

Strike like contempt.

Henry Timrod (1828–1867)

The Garden

This garden does not take my eyes,
Though here you show how art of men
Can purchase Nature at a price
Would stock old Paradise again.

These glories while you dote upon,
I envy not your spring nor pride,
Nay boast the summer all your own,
My thoughts with less are satisified.

Give me a little plot of ground,
Where might I with the sun agree,
Though every day he walk the round,
My garden he should seldom see.

Those tulips that such wealth display,
To court my eye, shall lose their name,
Though now they listen, as if they
Expected I should praise their flame.

But I would see myself appear
Within the violet's drooping head,
On which a melancholy tear
The discontented morn hath shed.

Within their buds let roses sleep,
And virgin lilies on their stem,
Till sighs from lovers glide and weep
Into their leaves to open them.

I' th' center of my ground compose
Of bays and yew my summer room,
Which may so oft as I repose,
Present my arbour, and my tomb.

No woman here shall find me out.
Or if a chance do bring one hither,
I'll be secure, for round about
I'll moat it with my eyes' foul weather.

No bird shall live within my pale.
To charm rue with their shames of art.
Unless some wandering nightingale
Come here to sing and break her heart.

Upon whose death I'll try to write
An epitaph, in some funeral stone.
So sad, and true, it may invite
Myself to die, and prove mine own.

James Shirley (1596-1666)

TREES

I think that I shall never see
A poem lovely as a tree.

A tree whose hungry mouth is prest
Against the earth's sweet flowing breast;

A tree that looks at God all day,
And lifts her leafy arms to pray;

A tree that may in Summer wear
A nest of robins in her hair;

Upon whose bosom snow has lain;
Who intimately lives with rain.

Poems are made by fools like me,
But only God can make a tree.

Joyce Kilmer (1886-1918)

ADAM AND EVE

When the first dark had fallen around them
And the leaves were weary of praise,
In the clear silence Beauty found them
And shewed them all her ways.

In the high noon of the heavenly garden
Where the angels sunned with the birds,
Beauty, before their hearts could harden,
Had taught them heavenly words.

When they fled in the burning weather
And nothing dawned but a dream,
Beauty fasted their hands together
And cooled them at her stream.

And when day wearied and night grew stronger,
And they slept as the beautiful must,
Then she bided a little longer,
And blossomed from their dust.

Marjorie Pickthall (1883-1922)

Lines Written in Kensington Gardens

In this lone, open glade I lie,
Screened by deep boughs on either hand;
And at its end, to stay the eye,
Those black-crowned, red-boled pine-trees stand.

Birds here make song, each bird has his,
Across the girdling city's hum.
How green under the boughs it is!
How thick the tremulous sheep-cries come!

Sometimes a child will cross the glade
To take his nurse his broken toy;
Sometimes a thrush flit overhead
Deep in her unknown day's employ.

Here at my feet what wonders pass!
What endless, active life is here!
What blowing daisies, fragrant grass!
An air-stirred forest, fresh and clear.

Scarce fresher is the mountain sod
Where the tired angler lies, stretched out,
And, eased of basket and of rod,
Counts his day's spoil, the spotted trout.

In the huge world which roars hard by,
Be others happy if they can!
But in my helpless cradle I
Was breathed on by the rural Pan.

I, on men's impious uproar hurled,
Think often, as I hear them rave,
That peace has left the upper world,
And now keeps only in the grave.

Yet here is peace forever new!
When I who watch them am away,
Still all things in this glade go through
The changes of their quiet day.

Then to their happy rest they pass;
The flowers upclose, the birds are fed,
The night comes down upon the grass,
The child sleeps warmly in his bed.

Calm soul of all things! make it mine
To feel, amid the city's jar,
That there abides a peace of thine,
Man did not make, and cannot mar.

The will to neither strive nor cry,
The power to feel with others, give!
Calm, calm me more! nor let me die
Before I have begun to live.

Matthew Arnold (1822-1888)

THE GARDEN

The issue of great Jove, draw near you, Muses nine:
Help us to praise the blissful plot of garden ground so fine.
The garden gives good food, and aid for leech's cure:
The garden, full of great delight, his master doth allure.
Sweet sallet herbs be here, and herbs of every kind;
The ruddy grapes, the seemly fruits be here at hand to find.
Here pleasance wanteth not, to make a man full fain:
Here marvelous the mixture is of solace, and of gain.
To water sundry seeds, the furrow by the way
A running river, trilling down with liquor, can convey.
Behold, with lively hue, fair flowers that shine so bright:
With riches, like the orient gems, they paint the mould in sight.
Bees, humming with soft sound, (their murmur is so small),
Of blooms and blossoms suck the tops, on dewed leaves they fall
The creeping vine holds down her own bewedded elms:
And, wandering out with branches thick, reeds
    folded overwhelms.
Trees spread their coverts wide, with shadows fresh and gay:
Full well their branched boughs defend the fervent sun away.
Birds chatter, and some chirp, and some sweet tunes do yield:

All mirthful, with their songs so blithe, they make both
    air and field.
The garden it allures, it feeds, it glads the sprite:
From heavy hearts all doleful dumps the garden chaseth quite.
Strength it restores to limbs, draws, and fulfills the sight:
with cheer revives the senses all, and maketh labour light.
O, what deights to us the garden ground doth bring?
Seed, leaf, flower, fruit, herb, bee, and tree & more than
    I may sing.

Nicholas Grimald (1519-1562)

GARDENER

True Bramin, in the morning meadows wet,
Expound the Vedas of the violet,
Or, hid in vines, peeping through many a loop,
See the plum redden, and the beurré stoop.

Ralph Waldo Emerson (1803-1882)

My Garden

If I could put my woods in song,
And tell what's there enjoyed,
All men would to my gardens throng,
And leave the cities void.

In my plot no tulips blow, –
Snow-loving pines and oaks instead;
And rank the savage maples grow
From spring's faint flush to autumn red.

My garden is a forest ledge
Which older forests bound;
The banks slope down to the blue lake-edge,
Then plunge to depths profound.

Here once the Deluge ploughed,
Laid the terraces, one by one;
Ebbing later whence it flowed,
They bleach and dry in the sun.

The sowers made haste to depart, –
The wind and the birds which sowed it;
Not for fame, nor by rules of art,
Planted these, and tempests flowed it.

Waters that wash my garden side
Play not in Nature's lawful web,
They heed not moon or solar tide, –
Five years elapse from flood to ebb.

Hither hasted, in old time, Jove,
And every god, – none did refuse;
And be sure at last came Love,
And after Love, the Muse.

Keen ears can catch a syllable,
As if one spake to another,
In the hemlocks tall, untameable,
And what the whispering grasses smother.

Æolian harps in the pine
Ring with the song of the Fates;
Infant Bacchus in the vine, –
Far distant yet his chorus waits.

Cast thou copy in verse one chime
Of the wood-bell's peal and cry,
Write in a book the morning's prime,
Or match with words that tender sky?

Wonderful verse of the gods,
Of one import, of varied tone;
They chant the bliss of their abodes
To man imprisoned in his own.

Ever the words of the gods resound;
But the porches of man's ear
Seldom in this low life's round
Are unsealed, that he may hear.

Wandering voices in the air,
And murmurs in the wold,
Speak what I cannot declare,
Yet cannot all withhold.

When the shadow fell on the lake,
The whirlwind in ripples wrote
Air-bells of fortune that shine and break,
And omens above thought.

But the meanings cleave to the lake,
Cannot be carried in book or urn;
Go thy ways now, come later back,
On waves and hedges still they burn.

These the fates of men forecast,
Of better men than live to-day;
If who can read them comes at last,
He will spell in the sculpture, 'Stay!'

Ralph Waldo Emerson (1803-1882)

The Glory of the Garden

Our England is a garden that is full of stately views,
Of borders, beds and shrubberies and lawns and avenues,
With statues on the terraces and peacocks strutting by;
But the Glory of the Garden lies in more than meets the eye.

For where the thick laurels grow, along the thin red wall,
You will find the tool- and potting-sheds which are the
    heart of all;
The cold-frames and the hot-houses, the dungpits and the tanks,
The rollers, carts and drain-pipes, with the barrows and
    the planks.

And there you'll see the gardners, the men and 'prentice boys
Told off to do as they are bid and to it without noise;
For, except when seeds are planted and we shout to
    scare the birds,
    The Glory of the Garden it abideth not in words.

And some can pot begonias and some can bud a rose,
And some are hardly fit to trust with anything that grows;

But they can roll and trim the lawns and sift the sand and loam,
For the Glory of the Garden occupieth all who come.

Our England is a garden, and such gardens are not made
By singing: – "Oh, how beautiful!" and sitting in the shade,
While better men than we go out and start their working lives
At grubbing weeds from gravel-paths with broken dinner-
knives.

There's not a pair of legs so thin, there's not a head so thick,
There's not a hand so weak and white, nor yet a heart so sick,
But it can find some needful job that's crying to be done,
For the Glory of the Garden glorifieth every one.

Then seek your job with thankfulness and work till
     further orders,
It it's only netting strawberries or killing slugs on borders;
And when your back stops aching and your hands begin
     to harden,
You will find yourself a partner in the Glory of the Garden.

Oh, Adam was a gardener, and God who made him sees

That half a proper gardener's work is done upon his knees,

So when your work is finished, you can wash your hands
     and pray

For the Glory of the Garden, that it may not pass away!

For the Glory of the Garden, that it may not pass away!

Rudyard Kipling (1865-1936)

This Lime-tree Bower my Prison

Well, they are gone, and here must I remain,
This lime-tree bower my prison! I have lost
Beauties and feelings, such as would have been
Most sweet to my remembrance even when age
Had dimm'd mine eyes to blindness! They, meanwhile,
Friends, whom I never more may meet again,
On springy heath, along the hill-top edge,
Wander in gladness, and wind down, perchance,
To that still roaring dell, of which I told;
The roaring dell, o'erwooded, narrow, deep,
And only speckled by the mid-day sun;
Where its slim trunk the ash from rock to rock
Flings arching like a bridge; – that branchless ash,
Unsunn'd and damp, whose few poor yellow leaves
Ne'er tremble in the gale, yet tremble still,
Fann'd by the water-fall! and there my friends
Behold the dark green file of long lank weeds,
That all at once (a most fantastic sight!)
Still nod and drip beneath the dripping edge
Of the blue clay-stone.

Now, my friends emerge

Beneath the wide wide Heaven – and view again

The many-steepled tract magnificent

Of hilly fields and meadows, and the sea,

With some fair bark, perhaps, whose sails light up

The slip of smooth clear blue betwixt two Isles

Of purple shadow! Yes! they wander on

In gladness all; but thou, methinks, most glad,

My gentle-hearted Charles! for thou hast pined

And hunger'd after Nature, many a year,

In the great City pent, winning thy way

With sad yet patient soul, through evil and pain

And strange calamity! Ah! slowly sink

Behind the western ridge, thou glorious Sun!

Shine in the slant beams of the sinking orb,

Ye purple heath-flowers! richlier burn, ye clouds!

Live in the yellow light, ye distant groves!

And kindle, thou blue Ocean! So my friend

Struck with deep joy may stand, as I have stood,

Silent with swimming sense; yea, gazing round

On the wide landscape, gaze till all doth seem

Less gross than bodily; and of such hues

As veil the Almighty Spirit, when yet he makes

Spirits perceive his presence.

A delight

Comes sudden on my heart, and I am glad

As I myself were there! Nor in this bower,

This little lime-tree bower, have I not mark'd

Much that has sooth'd me. Pale beneath the blaze

Hung the transparent foliage; and I watch'd

Some broad and sunny leaf, and lov'd to see

The shadow of the leaf and stem above

Dappling its sunshine! And that walnut-tree

Was richly ting'd, and a deep radiance lay

Full on the ancient ivy, which usurps

Those fronting elms, and now, with blackest mass

Makes their dark branches gleam a lighter hue

Through the late twilight: and though now the bat

Wheels silent by, and not a swallow twitters,

Yet still the solitary humble-bee

Sings in the bean-flower! Henceforth I shall know

That Nature ne'er deserts the wise and pure;

No plot so narrow, be but Nature there,

No waste so vacant, but may well employ

Each faculty of sense, and keep the heart

Awake to Love and Beauty! and sometimes

'Tis well to be bereft of promis'd good,

That we may lift the soul, and contemplate

With lively joy the joys we cannot share.
My gentle-hearted Charles! when the last rook
Beat its straight path across the dusky air
Homewards, I blest it! deeming its black wing
(Now a dim speck, now vanishing in light)
Had cross'd the mighty Orb's dilated glory,
While thou stood'st gazing; or, when all was still,
Flew creeking o'er thy head, and had a charm
For thee, my gentle-hearted Charles, to whom
No sound is dissonant which tells of Life.

Samuel Taylor Coleridge (1772–1834)

At Home from Church

The lilacs in the sunshine lift
Their plumes of dear old-fashioned flowers
Whose fragrance fills the silent house
Where, left alone, I count the hours.

High in the apple-trees the bees
Are humming, busy in the sun;
An idle robin cries for rain
But once or twice, and then is done.

The Sunday morning stillness holds
In heavy slumber all the street,
While from the church just out of sight
Behind the elms, comes slow and sweet

The organ's drone, the voices faint
That sing the quaint long-metre hymn–
I somehow feel as if shut out
From some mysterious temple, dim

And beautiful with blue and red
And golden lights from windows high,
Where angels in the shadows stand,
And earth seems very near the sky.

The day-dream fades, and so I try
Again to catch the tune that brings
No thought of temple or of priest,
But only of a voice that sings.

Sarah Orne Jewett (1849-1909)

THIS COMPOST

1

Something startles me where I thought I was safest,

I withdraw from the still woods I loved,

I will not go now on the pastures to walk,

I will not strip the clothes from my body to meet

    my lover the sea,

I will not touch my flesh to the earth as to other flesh

    to renew me.

O how can it be that the ground itself does not sicken?

How can you be alive you growths of spring?

How can you furnish health you blood of herbs, roots,

    orchards, grain?

Are they not continually putting distemper'd corpses

    within you?

Is not every continent work'd over and over with sour dead?

Where have you disposed of their carcasses?

Those drunkards and gluttons of so many generations?

Where have you drawn off all the foul liquid and meat?

I do not see any of it upon you to-day, or perhaps

    I am deceiv'd,

I will run a furrow with my plough, I will press my spade
      through the sod and turn it up underneath,
I am sure I shall expose some of the foul meat.

2

Behold this compost! behold it well!
Perhaps every mite has once form'd part of a sick
      person – yet behold!
The grass of spring covers the prairies,
The bean bursts noiselessly through the mould
      in the garden,
The delicate spear of the onion pierces upward,
The apple-buds cluster together on the apple-branches,
The resurrection of the wheat appears with pale visage
      out of its graves,
The tinge awakes over the willow-tree and the
      mulberry-tree,
The he-birds carol mornings and evenings while the she-
      birds sit on their nests,
The young of poultry break through the hatch'd eggs,
The new-born of animals appear, the calf is dropt from the
      cow, the colt from the mare,

Out of its little hill faithfully rise the potato's dark
    green leaves,
Out of its hill rises the yellow maize-stalk, the lilacs bloom
    in the dooryards,
The summer growth is innocent and disdainful above all
    those strata of sour dead.

What chemistry!
That the winds are really not infectious,
That this is no cheat, this transparent green-wash of the
    sea which is so amorous after me,
That it is safe to allow it to lick my naked body all
    over with its tongues,
That it will not endanger me with the fevers that have
    deposited themselves in it,
That all is clean forever and forever,
That the cool drink from the well tastes so good,
That blackberries are so flavorous and juicy,
That the fruits of the apple-orchard and the orange-orchard
    – that melons, grapes, peaches, plums, will none of them
    poison me,
That when I recline on the grass I do not catch any disease,

Though probably every spear of grass rises out of what was once a catching disease.

Now I am terrified at the Earth, it is that calm and patient,
It grows such sweet things out of such corruptions,
It turns harmless and stainless on its axis, with such endless
    successions of diseas'd corpses,
It distills such exquisite winds out of such infused fetor,
It renews with such unwitting looks its prodigal, annual,
    sumptuous crops,
It gives such divine materials to men, and accepts such
    leavings from them at last.

Walt Whitman (1819-1892)

THE GARDEN OF LOVE

I went to the Garden of Love,
And saw what I never had seen;
A Chapel was built in the midst,
Where I used to play on the green.

And the gates of this Chapel were shut,
And 'Thou shalt not' writ over the door;
So I turned to the Garden of Love
That so many sweet flowers bore.

And I saw it was filled with graves,
And tombstones where flowers should be;
And priests in black gowns were walking their rounds,
And binding with briars my joys and desires.

William Blake (1757–1827)

Lines Written in Early Spring

I heard a thousand blended notes,
While in a grove I sate reclined,
In that sweet mood when pleasant thoughts
Bring sad thoughts to the mind.

To her fair works did nature link
The human soul that through me ran;
And much it griev'd my heart to think
What man has made of man.

Through primrose tufts, in that sweet bower,
The periwinkle trail'd its wreathes;
And 'tis my faith that every flower
Enjoys the air it breathes.

The birds around me hopp'd and play'd:
Their thoughts I cannot measure,
But the least motion which they made,
It seem'd a thrill of pleasure.

The budding twigs spread out their fan,
To catch the breezy air;
And I must think, do all I can,
That there was pleasure there.

If I these thoughts may not prevent,
If such be of my creed the plan,
Have I not reason to lament
What man has made of man?

William Wordsworth (1770-1850)

Changing Seasons
and Passing of Time

Memory, Decay, and Regeneration

A Shropshire Lad 2

Loveliest of trees, the cherry now
Is hung with bloom along the bough,
And stands about the woodland ride
Wearing white for Eastertide.

Now, of my threescore years and ten,
Twenty will not come again,
And take from seventy springs a score,
It only leaves me fifty more.

And since to look at things in bloom
Fifty springs are little room,
About the woodlands I will go
To see the cherry hung with snow.

A.E. Housman (1859–1936)

A Forsaken Garden

In a coign of the cliff between lowland and highland,
At the sea-down's edge between windward and lee,
Walled round with rocks as an inland island,
The ghost of a garden fronts the sea.
A girdle of brushwood and thorn encloses
The steep square slope of the blossomless bed
Where the weeds that grew green from the graves of its roses
Now lie dead.

The fields fall southward, abrupt and broken,
To the low last edge of the long lone land.
If a step should sound or a word be spoken,
Would a ghost not rise at the strange guest's hand?
So long have the grey bare walks lain guestless,
Through branches and briars if a man make way,
He shall find no life but the sea-wind's, restless
Night and day.

The dense hard passage is blind and stifled
That crawls by a track none turn to climb
To the strait waste place that the years have rifled

Of all but the thorns that are touched not of time.
The thorns he spares when the rose is taken;
The rocks are left when he wastes the plain.
The wind that wanders, the weeds wind-shaken,
These remain.

Not a flower to be pressed of the foot that falls not;
As the heart of a dead man the seed-plots are dry;
From the thicket of thorns whence the nightingale calls not,
Could she call, there were never a rose to reply.
Over the meadows that blossom and wither
Rings but the note of a sea-bird's song;
Only the sun and the rain come hither
All year long.

The sun burns sere and the rain dishevels
One gaunt bleak blossom of scentless breath.
Only the wind here hovers and revels
In a round where life seems barren as death.
Here there was laughing of old, there was weeping,
Haply, of lovers none ever will know,
Whose eyes went seaward a hundred sleeping
Years ago.

Heart handfast in heart as they stood, "Look thither,"
Did he whisper? "look forth from the flowers to the sea;
For the foam-flowers endure when the rose-blossoms wither,
And men that love lightly may die – but we?"
And the same wind sang and the same waves whitened,
And or ever the garden's last petals were shed,
In the lips that had whispered, the eyes that had lightened,
Love was dead.

Or they loved their life through, and then went whither?
And were one to the end – but what end who knows?
Love deep as the sea as a rose must wither,
As the rose-red seaweed that mocks the rose.
Shall the dead take thought for the dead to love them?
What love was ever as deep as a grave?
They are loveless now as the grass above them
Or the wave.

All are at one now, roses and lovers,
Not known of the cliffs and the fields and the sea.
Not a breath of the time that has been hovers
In the air now soft with a summer to be.
Not a breath shall there sweeten the seasons hereafter

Of the flowers or the lovers that laugh now or weep,

When as they that are free now of weeping and laughter

We shall sleep.

Here death may deal not again for ever;

Here change may come not till all change end.

From the graves they have made they shall rise up never,

Who have left nought living to ravage and rend.

Earth, stones, and thorns of the wild ground growing,

While the sun and the rain live, these shall be;

Till a last wind's breath upon all these blowing

Roll the sea.

Till the slow sea rise and the sheer cliff crumble,

Till terrace and meadow the deep gulfs drink,

Till the strength of the waves of the high tides humble

The fields that lessen, the rocks that shrink,

Here now in his triumph where all things falter,

Stretched out on the spoils that his own hand spread,

As a god self-slain on his own strange altar,

Death lies dead.

Algernon Charles Swinburne (1837–1909)

The Fruit Garden Path

The path runs straight between the flowering rows,
A moonlit path, hemmed in by beds of bloom,
Where phlox and marigolds dispute for room
With tall, red dahlias and the briar rose.
'T is reckless prodigality which throws
Into the night these wafts of rich perfume
Which sweep across the garden like a plume.
Over the trees a single bright star glows.
Dear garden of my childhood, here my years
Have run away like little grains of sand;
The moments of my life, its hopes and fears
Have all found utterance here, where now I stand;
My eyes ache with the weight of unshed tears,
You are my home, do you not understand?

Amy Lowell (1874-1925)

SONNET 84

While one sere leaf, that parting Autumn gilds,
Trembles upon the thin, and naked spray,
November, dragging on his sunless day,
Lours, cold and fallen, on the watry fields;
And Nature to the waste dominion yields,
Stript her last robes, with gold and purple gay –
So droops my life, of your soft beams despoil'd,
Youth, Health, and Hope, that long exulting smil'd;
And the wild carols, and the bloomy hues
Of merry Spring-time, spruce on every plain
Her half-blown bushes, moist with sunny rain,
More pensive thoughts in my sunk heart infuse
Than Winter's grey, and desolate domain,
Faded, like my lost Youth, that no bright Spring renews.

Anna Seward (1742-1809)

SONNET 92

Behold that Tree, in Autumn's dim decay,
Stript by the frequent, chill, and eddying Wind;
Where yet some yellow, lonely leaves we find
Lingering and trembling on the naked spray,
Twenty, perchance, for millions whirl'd away!
Emblem, alas! too just, of Humankind!
Vain Man expects longevity, design'd
For few indeed; and their protracted day
What is it worth that Wisdom does not scorn?
The blasts of Sickness, Care, and Grief appal,
That laid the Friends in dust, whose natal morn
Rose near their own; – and solemn is the call; –
Yet, like those weak, deserted leaves forlorn,
Shivering they cling to life, and fear to fall!

Anna Seward (1742-1809)

Sonnet 36: Summer

Now on hills, rocks, and streams, and vales, and plains,
Full looks the shining Day. – Our gardens wear
The gorgeous robes of the consummate Year.
With laugh, and shout, and song, stout Maids and Swains
Heap high the fragrant hay, as thro' rough lanes
Rings the yet empty waggon. – See in air
The pendent cherries, red with tempting stains,
Gleam thro' their boughs. – Summer, thy bright career
Must slacken soon in Autumn's milder sway;
Then thy now heapt and jocund meads shall stand
Smooth, – vacant, – silent, – thro' th' exulting Land
As wave thy Rival's golden fields, and gay
Her Reapers throng. She smiles, and binds the sheaves;
Then bends her parting step o'er fall'n and rustling leaves.

Anna Seward (1742-1809)

THE GARDEN OF THE PALAIS ROYAL

In the Palais Royal by moonlight,
Watching the fountains play,
Are a thousand ghostly shadows
Of those who are passed away.
Shadows of beauty and splendour,
Flitting from salle to salle;
Sweetest of all among them,
Marie Thérèse de Lamballe!

Yet there is not a place in Paris
Where it seems less wise to dream,
Than here, where the people gather
And flow in an endless stream;
Full of their follies and pleasures,
Full of the last new thing,
Under the close-cropped lindens,
Blossoming every spring.

But for me the Palais Royal
Is full of the days gone by,
And the flash of the silver fountains
Is a murmur blent with a sigh;
And the steps of the people passing
Are as if they came to me
From the far, unearthly distance
Of a bygone century!

Bessie Rayner Parkes (1829–1925)

The Trees Are Down

—and he cried with a loud voice:
Hurt not the earth, neither the sea, nor the trees —
(Revelation)

They are cutting down the great plane-trees at the end
    of the gardens.
For days there has been the grate of the saw, the swish of
    the branches as they fall,
The crash of the trunks, the rustle of trodden leaves,
With the 'Whoops' and the 'Whoas,' the loud common
    talk, the loud common laughs of the men, above it all.

I remember one evening of a long past Spring
Turning in at a gate, getting out of a cart, and finding
    a large dead rat in the mud of the drive.
I remember thinking: alive or dead, a rat was a
    god-forsaken thing,
But at least, in May, that even a rat should be alive.

The week's work here is as good as done. There is just one bough
On the roped bole, in the fine grey rain,

Green and high

And lonely against the sky.

(Down now! –)

And but for that,

If an old dead rat

Did once, for a moment, unmake the Spring, I might never
have thought of him again.

It is not for a moment the Spring is unmade to-day;

These were great trees, it was in them from root to stem:

When the men with the 'Whoops' and the 'Whoas' have
carted the whole of the whispering loveliness away

Half the Spring, for me, will have gone with them.

It is going now, and my heart has been struck with the
hearts of the planes;

Half my life it has beat with these, in the sun, in the rains,

In the March wind, the May breeze,

In the great gales that came over to them across the roofs
from the great seas.

There was only a quiet rain when they were dying;

They must have heard the sparrows flying,
And the small creeping creatures in the earth where they
    were lying –
But I, all day, I heard an angel crying:
'Hurt not the trees.'

Charlotte Mew (1869–1928)

FALL, LEAVES, FALL

Fall, leaves, fall; die, flowers, away;
Lengthen night and shorten day;
Every leaf speaks bliss to me,
Fluttering from the autumn tree.
I shall smile when wreaths of snow
Blossom where the rose should grow;
I shall sing when night's decay
Ushers in a drearier day.

Emily Brontë (1818–1848)

NEW FEET WITHIN MY GARDEN GO

New feet within my garden go –
New fingers stir the sod –
A Troubadour upon the Elm
Betrays the solitude.

New children play upon the green –
New Weary sleep below –
And still the pensive Spring returns –
And still the punctual snow!

Emily Dickinson (1830-1886)

MAY-FLOWER

Pink, small, and punctual,
Aromatic, low,
Covert in April,
Candid in May,

Dear to the moss,
Known by the knoll,
Next to the robin
In every human soul.

Bold little beauty,
Bedecked with thee,
Nature forswears
Antiquity.

Emily Dickinson (1830-1886)

THE GRASS

The grass so little has to do, –
A sphere of simple green,
With only butterflies to brood,
And bees to entertain,

And stir all day to pretty tunes
The breezes fetch along,
And hold the sunshine in its lap
And bow to everything;

And thread the dews all night, like pearls,
And make itself so fine, –
A duchess were too common
For such a noticing.

And even when it dies, to pass
In odors so divine,
As lowly spices gone to sleep,
Or amulets of pine.

And then to dwell in sovereign barns,
And dream the days away, –
The grass so little has to do,
I wish I were the hay!

Emily Dickinson (1830-1886)

CHARLOTTE BRONTË'S GRAVE

All overgrown by cunning moss,
All interspersed with weed,
The little cage of 'Currer Bell,'
In quiet Haworth laid.

This bird, observing others,
When frosts too sharp became,
Retire to other latitudes,
Quietly did the same,

But differed in returning;
Since Yorkshire hills are green,
Yet not in all the nests I meet
Can nightingale be seen.

Gathered from many wanderings,
Gethsemane can tell
Through what transporting anguish
She reached the asphodel!

Soft fall the sounds of Eden
Upon her puzzled ear;
Oh, what an afternoon for heaven,
When 'Brontë' entered there!

Emily Dickinson (1830-1886)

The Autumnal Rose-Bud

Come out, pretty Rose-Bud, my lone, timid one!
Come forth from thy green leaves, and peep at the sun;
For little he does, in these dull autumn hours,
At height'ning of beauty, or laughing with flowers.

His beams, on thy tender young cheek as he plays,
Will give it a blush that no other can raise;
Thy fine silken petals they 'll softly unfold,
And fill their pure centre with spices and gold.

I would not instruct thee in coveting wealth;
But beauty, we know, is the offspring of health;
And health, the fair daughter of freedom, is bright
With feasting on breezes, and drinking the light.

Then come, pretty bud; from thy covert look out,
And see what the glad, golden sun is about:
His shafts, should they strike thee, will only impart
A grace to thy form, and a sweet to thy heart.

Hannah F. Gould (1789-1865)

FLOOD-TIDE OF FLOWERS

In Holland

The laggard winter ebbed so slow
With freezing rain and melting snow,
It seemed as if the earth would stay
Forever where the tide was low,
In sodden green and watery gray.

But now from depths beyond our sight,
The tide is turning in the night,
And floods of color long concealed
Come silent rising toward the light,
Through garden bare and empty field.

And first, along the sheltered nooks,
The crocus runs in little brooks
Of joyance, till by light made bold
They show the gladness of their looks
In shining pools of white and gold.

The tiny scilla, sapphire blue,

Is gently sweeping in, to strew

The earth with heaven; and sudden rills

Of sunlit yellow, sweeping through,

Spread into lakes of daffodils.

The hyacinths, with fragrant heads,

Have overflowed their sandy beds,

And fill the earth with faint perfume,

The breath that Spring around her sheds.

And now the tulips break in bloom!

A sea, a rainbow-tinted sea,

A splendor and a mystery,

Floods o'er the fields of faded gray:

The roads are full of folks in glee,

For lo, – to-day is Easter Day!

Henry van Dyke (1852-1933)

THE CHILD IN THE GARDEN

When to the garden of untroubled thought
I came of late, and saw the open door,
And wished again to enter, and explore
The sweet, wild ways with stainless bloom inwrought,
And bowers of innocence with beauty fraught,
It seemed some purer voice must speak before
I dared to tread that garden loved of yore,
That Eden lost unknown and found unsought.

Then just within the gate I saw a child, –
A stranger-child, yet to my heart most dear;
He held his hands to me, and softly smiled
With eyes that knew no shade of sin or fear:
"Come in," he said, "and play awhile with me;
I am the little child you used to be."

Henry van Dyke (1852-1933)

Autumn in the Garden

When the frosty kiss of Autumn in the dark
Makes its mark
On the flowers, and the misty morning grieves
Over fallen leaves;
Then my olden garden, where the golden soil
Through the toil
Of a hundred years is mellow, rich, and deep,
Whispers in its sleep.

'Mid the crumpled beds of marigold and phlox,
Where the box
Borders with its glossy green the ancient walks,
There's a voice that talks
Of the human hopes that bloomed and withered here
Year by year, –
And the dreams that brightened all the labouring hours,
Fading as the flowers.

Yet the whispered story does not deepen grief;
But relief
For the loneliness of sorrow seems to flow
From the Long-Ago,
When I think of other lives that learned, like mine,
To resign,
And remember that the sadness of the fall
Comes alike to all.

What regrets, what longings for the lost were theirs
And what prayers
For the silent strength that nerves us to endure
Things we cannot cure!
Pacing up and down the garden where they paced,
I have traced
All their well-worn paths of patience, till I find
Comfort in my mind.

Faint and far away their ancient griefs appear:
Yet how near
Is the tender voice, the careworn, kindly face,
Of the human race!
Let us walk together in the garden, dearest heart, –
Not apart!
They who know the sorrows other lives have known
Never walk alone.

Henry van Dyke (1852-1933)

To Autumn

1

Season of mists and mellow fruitfulness,

Close bosom-friend of the maturing sun;

Conspiring with him how to load and bless

With fruit the vines that round the thatch-eves run;

To bend with apples the moss'd cottage-trees,

And fill all fruit with ripeness to the core;

To swell the gourd, and plump the hazel shells

With a sweet kernel; to set budding more,

And still more, later flowers for the bees,

Until they think warm days will never cease,

For Summer has o'er-brimm'd their clammy cells.

2

Who hath not seen thee oft amid thy store?

Sometimes whoever seeks abroad may find

Thee sitting careless on a granary floor,

Thy hair soft-lifted by the winnowing wind;

Or on a half-reap'd furrow sound asleep,

Drows'd with the fume of poppies, while thy hook

Spares the next swath and all its twined flowers:

And sometimes like a gleaner thou dost keep
Steady thy laden head across a brook;
Or by a cyder-press, with patient look,
Thou watchest the last oozings hours by hours.

3

Where are the songs of Spring? Ay, where are they?
Think not of them, thou hast thy music too, –
While barred clouds bloom the soft-dying day,
And touch the stubble-plains with rosy hue;
Then in a wailful choir the small gnats mourn
Among the river sallows, borne aloft
Or sinking as the light wind lives or dies;
And full-grown lambs loud bleat from hilly bourn;
Hedge-crickets sing; and now with treble soft
The red-breast whistles from a garden-croft;
And gathering swallows twitter in the skies.

John Keats (1795–1821)

The Gardener 85

Who are you, reader, reading my poems an hundred
  years hence?
I cannot send you one single flower from this wealth of the
  spring, one single streak of gold from yonder clouds.
Open your doors and look abroad.

From your blossoming garden gather fragrant memories of
  the vanished flowers of an hundred years before.
In the joy of your heart may you feel the living joy that
  sang one spring morning, sending its glad voice across
  an hundred years.

Rabindranath Tagore (1861-1941)

Days

Damsels of Time, the hypocritic Days,
Muffled and dumb like barefoot dervishes,
And marching single in an endless file,
Bring diadems and fagots in their hands.
To each they offer gifts after his will,
Bread, kingdoms, stars, and sky that holds them all.
I, in my pleached garden, watched the pomp,
Forgot my morning wishes, hastily
Took a few herbs and apples, and the Day
Turned and departed silent. I, too late,
Under her solemn fillet saw the scorn.

Ralph Waldo Emerson (1803-1882)

Autumn Fires

In the other gardens
And all up the vale,
From the autumn bonfires
See the smoke trail!

Pleasant summer over
And all the summer flowers,
The red fire blazes,
The grey smoke towers.

Sing a song of seasons!
Something bright in all!
Flowers in the summer,
Fires in the fall!

Robert Louis Stevenson (1850-1894)

GROWN ABOUT BY FRAGRANT BUSHES

There where the land of love,
Grown about by fragrant bushes,
Sunken in a winding valley,
Where the clear winds blow
And the shadows come and go,
And the cattle stand and low
And the sheep bells and the linnets
Sing and tinkle musically.
Between the past and the future,
Those two black infinities
Between which our brief life
Flashes a moment and goes out.

Robert Louis Stevenson (1850-1894)

The Garden Year

January brings the snow,
Makes our feet and fingers glow.

February brings the rain,
Thaws the frozen lake again.

March brings breezes, loud and shrill,
To stir the dancing daffodil.

April brings the primrose sweet,
Scatters daisies at our feet.

May brings flocks of pretty lambs
Skipping by their fleecy dams.

June brings tulips, lilies, roses,
Fills the children's hands with posies.

Hot July brings cooling showers,
Apricots, and gillyflowers.

August brings the sheaves of corn,
Then the harvest home is borne.

Warm September brings the fruit;
Sportsmen then begin to shoot.

Fresh October brings the pheasant;
Then to gather nuts is pleasant.

Dull November brings the blast;
Then the leaves are whirling fast.

Chill December brings the sleet,
Blazing fire, and Christmas treat.

Sara Coleridge (1802-1852)

In the Garden

We waited for the sun
To break its cloudy prison
(For day was not yet done,
And night still unbegun)
Leaning by the dial.

After many a trial –
We all silent there –
It burst as new-arisen,
Throwing a shade to where
Time travelled at that minute.

Little saw we in it,
But this much I know,
Of lookers on that shade,
Her towards whom it made
Soonest had to go.

Thomas Hardy (1840-1928)

Be still. The Hanging Gardens were a dream

Be still. The Hanging Gardens were a dream
That over Persian roses flew to kiss
The curlèd lashes of Semiramis.
Troy never was, nor green Skamander stream.
Provence and Troubadour are merest lies
The glorious hair of Venice was a beam
Made within Titian's eye. The sunsets seem,
The world is very old and nothing is.
Be still. Thou foolish thing, thou canst not wake,
Nor thy tears wedge thy soldered lids apart,
But patter in the darkness of thy heart.
Thy brain is plagued. Thou art a frighted owl
Blind with the light of life thou 'ldst not forsake,
And Error loves and nourishes thy soul.

Trumbull Stickney (1874–1904)

Loneliness

These autumn gardens, russet, gray and brown,
The sward with shrivelled foliage strown,
The shrubs and trees
By weary wings of sunshine overflown
And timid silences, –

Since first you, darling, called my spirit yours,
Seem happy, and the gladness pours
From day to day,
And yester-year across this year endures
Unto next year away.

Now in these places where I used to rove
And give the dropping leaves my love
And weep to them,
They seem to fall divinely from above,
Like to a diadem

Closing in one with the disheartened flowers.
High up the migrant birds in showers

Shine in the sky,

And all the movement of the natural hours

Turns into melody.

Trumbull Stickney (1874–1904)

SONNET

Alas, that June should come when thou didst go;
I think you passed each other on the way;
And seeing thee, the Summer loved thee so
That all her loveliness she gave away;
Her rare perfumes, in hawthorn boughs distilled,
Blushing, she in thy sweeter bosom left,
Thine arms with all her virgin roses filled,
Yet felt herself the richer for thy theft;
Beggared herself of morning for thine eyes,
Hung on the lips of every bird the tune,
Breathed on thy cheek her soft vermilion dyes,
And in thee set the singing heart of June.
And so, not only do I mourn thy flight,
But Summer comes despoiled of her delight.

Willa Cather (1873-1947)

GARDENS OF
THE SOUL

Love, Desire and Imagination

Come into the Garden, Maud (Extract, Maud, Part 1)

1

Come into the garden, Maud,

For the black bat, night, has flown,

Come into the garden, Maud,

I am here at the gate alone;

And the woodbine spices are wafted abroad,

And the musk of the roses blown.

2

For a breeze of morning moves,

And the planet of Love is on high,

Beginning to faint in the light that she loves

On a bed of daffodil sky,

To faint in the light of the sun she loves.

To faint in his light, and to die.

3

All night have the roses heard

The flute, violin, bassoon;

All night has the casement jessamine stirr'd

To the dangers dancing in tune;

Till a silence fell with the waking bird,
And a hush with the setting moon.

4

I said to the lily, 'There is but one
With whom she has heart to be gay.
When will the dancers leave her alone?
She is weary of dance and play.'
Now half to the setting moon are gone,
And half to the rising day;
Low on the sand and loud on the stone
The last wheel echoes away.

5

I said to the rose, 'The brief night goes
In babble and revel and wine.
young lord-lover, what sighs are those,
For one that will never be thine?
But mine, but mine,' so I sware to the rose,
'For ever and ever, mine.'

6

And the soul of the rose went into my blood,

As the music clash'd in the hall;

And long by the garden lake I stood.

For I heard your rivulet fall

From the lake to the meadow and on to the wood,

Our wood, that is dearer than all;

7

From the meadow your walks have left so sweet

That whenever a March-wind sighs

He sets the jewel-print of your feet

In violets blue as your eyes,

To the woody hollows in which we meet

And the valleys of Paradise.

8

The slender acacia would not shake

One long milk-bloom on the tree;

The white lake-blossom fell into the lake,

As the pimpernel dozed on the lea;
But the rose was awake all night for your sake,
Knowing your promise to me;
The lilies and roses were all awake.
They sigh'd for the dawn and thee.

9

Queen rose of the rosebud garden of girls,
Come hither, the dances are done,
In gloss of satin and glimmer of pearls,
Queen lily and rose in one;
Shine out, little head, sunning over with curls,
To the flowers, and be their sun.

10

There has fallen a splendid tear
From the passion-flower at the gate.
She is coming, my dove, my dear;
She is coming, my life, my fate;
The red rose cries, *She is near, she is near;'
And the white rose weeps, 'She is late;'
The larkspur listens, 'I hear, I hear;'
And the lily whispers, 'I wait.'

11

She is coming, my own, my sweet;

Were it ever so airy a tread.

My heart would hear her and beat,

Were it earth in an earthy bed;

My dust would hear her and beat,

Had I lain for a century dead;

Would start and tremble under her feet,

And blossom in purple and red.

Alfred, Lord Tennyson (1809-1892)

Now Sleeps the Crimson Petal
(Extract, The Princess, Part 7)

Now sleeps the crimson petal, now the white;
Nor waves the cypress in the palace walk;
Nor winks the gold fin in the porphyry font.
The firefly wakens; waken thou with me.

Now droops the milk-white peacock like a ghost,
And like a ghost she glimmers on to me.

Now lies the Earth all Danaë to the stars,
And all thy heart lies open unto me.

Now slides the silent meteor on, and leaves
A shining furrow, as thy thoughts in me.

Now folds the lily all her sweetness up,
And slips into the bosom of the lake.
So fold thyself, my dearest, thou, and slip
Into my bosom and be lost in me.

Alfred, Lord Tennyson (1809-1892)

In a Garden

Gushing from the mouths of stone men
To spread at ease under the sky
In granite-lipped basins,
Where iris dabble their feet
And rustle to a passing wind,
The water fills the garden with its rushing,
In the midst of the quiet of close-clipped lawns.

Damp smell the ferns in tunnels of stone,
Where trickle and plash the fountains,
Marble fountains, yellowed with much water.

Splashing down moss-tarnished steps
It falls, the water;
And the air is throbbing with it.
With its gurgling and running.
With its leaping, and deep, cool murmur.

And I wished for night and you.
I wanted to see you in the swimming-pool,
White and shining in the silver-flecked water.

While the moon rode over the garden,

High in the arch of night,

And the scent of the lilacs was heavy with stillness.

Night, and the water, and you in your whiteness, bathing!

Amy Lowell (1874-1925)

The Garden by Moonlight

A black cat among roses,
Phlox, lilac-misted under a first-quarter moon,
The sweet smells of heliotrope and night-scented stock.
The garden is very still,
It is dazed with moonlight,
Contented with perfume,
Dreaming the opium dreams of its folded poppies.
Firefly lights open and vanish
High as the tip buds of the golden glow
Low as the sweet alyssum flowers at my feet.
Moon-shimmer on leaves and trellises,
Moon-spikes shafting through the snowball bush.
Only the little faces of the ladies' delight are alert
    and staring,
Only the cat, padding between the roses,
Shakes a branch and breaks the chequered pattern
As water is broken by the falling of a leaf.
Then you come,
And you are quiet like the garden,
And white like the alyssum flowers,
And beautiful as the silent sparks of the fireflies.

Ah, Beloved, do you see those orange lilies?
They knew my mother,
But who belonging to me will they know
When I am gone.

Amy Lowell (1874-1925)

Behind a Wall

I own a solace shut within my heart,
A garden full of many a quaint delight
And warm with drowsy, poppied sunshine; bright,
Flaming with lilies out of whose cups dart
Shining things
With powdered wings.

Here terrace sinks to terrace, arbors close
The ends of dreaming paths; a wanton wind
Jostles the half-ripe pears, and then, unkind,
Tumbles a-slumber in a pillar rose,
With content
Grown indolent.

By night my garden is o'erhung with gems
Fixed in an onyx setting. Fireflies
Flicker their lanterns in my dazzled eyes.
In serried rows I guess the straight, stiff stems
Of hollyhocks
Against the rocks.

So far and still it is that, listening,
I hear the flowers talking in the dawn;
And where a sunken basin cuts the lawn,
Cinctured with iris, pale and glistening,
The sudden swish
Of a waking fish.

Amy Lowell (1874-1925)

The Mower Against Gardens

Luxurious man, to bring his vice in use,
Did after him the world seduce,
And from the fields the flowers and plants allure,
Where Nature was most plain and pure.
He first inclosed within the gardens square
A dead and standing pool of air,
And a more luscious earth for them did knead,
Which stupefied them while it fed.
The pink grew then as double as his mind;
The nutriment did change the kind.
With strange perfumes he did the roses taint;
And flowers themselves were taught to paint.
The tulip white did for complexion seek,
And learned to interline its cheek;
Its onion root they then so high did hold,
That one was for a meadow sold:
Another world was searched through oceans new,
To find the marvel of Peru;
And yet these rarities might be allowed
To man, that sovereign thing and proud,
Had he not dealt between the bark and tree,

Forbidden mixtures there to see.

No plant now knew the stock from which it came;

He grafts upon the wild the tame,

That the uncertain and adulterate fruit

Might put the palate in dispute.

His green seraglio has its eunuchs too,

Lest any tyrant him outdo;

And in the cherry he does Nature vex,

To procreate without a sex.

'Tis all enforced, the fountain and the grot,

While the sweet fields do lie forgot,

Where willing Nature does to all dispense

A wild and fragrant innocence;

And fauns and fairies do the meadows till

More by their presence than their skill.

Their statues polished by some ancient hand,

May to adorn the gardens stand;

But, howsoe'er the figures do excel,

The Gods themselves with us do dwell.

Andrew Marvell (1621-1678)

Sonnet 44

Beloved, thou hast brought me many flowers

Plucked in the garden, all the summer through

And winter, and it seemed as if they grew

In this close room, nor missed the sun and showers,

So, in the like name of that love of ours,

Take back these thoughts which here unfolded too,

And which on warm and cold days I withdrew

From my heart's ground. Indeed, those beds and bowers

Be overgrown with bitter weeds and rue,

And wait thy weeding; yet here's eglantine,

Here's ivy! – take them, as I used to do

Thy flowers, and keep them where they shall not pine.

Instruct thine eyes to keep their colours true,

And tell thy soul, their roots are left in mine.

Elizabeth Barrett Browning (1806-1861)

Apotheosis

Come slowly, Eden!
Lips unused to thee,
Bashful, sip thy jasmines,
As the fainting bee,

Reaching late his flower,
Round her chamber hums,
Counts his nectars – enters,
And is lost in balms!

Emily Dickinson (1830-1886)

Have you got a brook in your little heart

Have you got a brook in your little heart,
Where bashful flowers blow,
And blushing birds go down to drink,
And shadows tremble so?

And nobody knows, so still it flows,
That any brook is there;
And yet your little draught of life
Is daily drunken there.

Then look out for the little brook in March,
When the rivers overflow,
And the snows come hurrying from the hills,
And the bridges often go.

And later, in August it may be,
When the meadows parching lie,
Beware, lest this little brook of life
Some burning noon go dry!

Emily Dickinson (1830-1886)

I HAVE NOT TOLD MY GARDEN YET

I have not told my garden yet,
Lest that should conquer me;
I have not quite the strength now
To break it to the bee.

I will not name it in the street,
For shops would stare, that I,
So shy, so very ignorant,
Should have the face to die.

The hillsides must not know it,
Where I have rambled so,
Nor tell the loving forests
The day that I shall go,

Nor lisp it at the table,
Nor heedless by the way
Hint that within the riddle
One will walk to-day!

Emily Dickinson (1830-1886)

RENCONTRE

Oh, was I born too soon, my dear, or were you born too late,
That I am going out the door while you come in the gate?
For you the garden blooms galore, the castle is en fête;
You are the coming guest, my dear, – for me the horses wait.

I know the mansion well, my dear, its rooms so rich
    and wide;
If you had only come before I might have been your guide,
And hand in hand with you explore the treasures that
    they hide;
But you have come to stay, my dear, and I prepare to ride.

Then walk with me an hour, my dear, and pluck the
    reddest rose
Amid the white and crimson store with which your
    garden glows, –
A single rose, – I ask no more of what your love bestows;
It is enough to give, my dear, – a flower to him who goes.

The House of Life is yours, my dear, for many and many a day,
But I must ride the lonely shore, the Road to Far Away:

So bring the stirrup-cup and pour a brimming draught, I pray,

And when you take the road, my dear, I'll meet you on
the way.

Henry van Dyke (1852-1933)

THE LADY JANE (EXTRACT, THE KINGIS QUAIR)

Bewailing in my chamber, thus alone,
Despaired of all joy and remedy,
For-tired of my thought, and woe-begone,
And to the window gan I walk in hy
To see the world and folk that went forbye
As, for the time, though I of mirthis food
Might have no more, to look it did me good.

Now was there made, fast by the towris wall,
A garden fair; and in the corners set
Ane arbour green, with wandis long and small
Railed about, and so with trees set
Was all the place, and hawthorn hedges knet
That lyf was none walking there forbye,
That might within scarce any wight espy.

So thick the boughis and the leavis green
Beshaded all the alleys that there were,
And mids of every arbour might be seen
The sharpe greene sweete juniper,
Growing so fair with branches here and there,

That as it seemed to a lyf without,
The boughis spread the arbour all about.

And on the smalle greene twistis sat,
The little sweete nightingale, and sung
So loud and clear, the hymnis consecrat
Of lovis use, now soft, now loud among,
That all the gardens and the wallis rung
Right of their song.

And therewith cast I down mine eyes again,
Where as I saw, walking under the tower,
Full secretly, new comen here to plain,
The fairist or the freshest younge flower
That ever I saw, methought, before that hour,
For which sudden abate, anon astart,
The blood of all my body to my heart.

And though I stood abasit tho a lite,
No wonder was; for why? my wittis all
Were so overcome with pleasance and delight,
Only through letting of my eyen fall,
That suddenly my heart became her thrall,

For ever of free will, – for of menace
There was no token in her sweete face.

And in my head I drew right hastily,
And eftesoons I leant it out again,
And saw her walk that very womanly,
With no wight mo', but only women twain.
Then gan I study in myself, and sayn,
"Ah, sweet! are ye a worldly creature,
Or heavenly thing in likeness of nature?

"Or are ye god Cupidis own princess,
And comin are to loose me out of band?
Or are ye very Nature the goddess,
That have depainted with your heavenly hand,
This garden full of flowers as they stand?
What shall I think, alas! what reverence
Shall I mister unto your excellence?

"If ye a goddess be, and that ye like
To do me pain, I may it not astart:
If ye be warldly wight, that doth me sike,
Why list God make you so, my dearest heart,

To do a seely prisoner this smart,
That loves you all, and wot of nought but wo?
And therefore mercy, sweet! sin' it is so."

Of her array the form if I shall write,
Towards her golden hair and rich attire,
In fretwise couchit with pearlis white
And great balas leaming as the fire,
With mony ane emeraut and fair sapphire;
And on her head a chaplet fresh of hue,
Of plumis parted red, and white, and blue.

Full of quaking spangis bright as gold,
Forged of shape like to the amorets,
So new, so fresh, so pleasant to behold,
The plumis eke like to the flower jonets;
And other of shape like to the flower jonets;
And above all this, there was, well I wot,
Beauty enough to make a world to doat.

About her neck, white as the fire amail,
A goodly chain of small orfevory,

Whereby there hung a ruby, without fail,
Like to ane heart shapen verily,
That as asp ark of low, so wantonly
Seemed burning upon her white throat,
Now if there was good party, God it wot.

And for to walk that fresh May's morrow,
Ane hook she had upon her tissue white,
That goodlier had not been seen to-forow,
As I suppose; and girt she was alite,
Thus halflings loose for haste, to such delight
It was to see her youth in goodlihede,
That for rudeness to speak thereof I dread.

In her was youth, beauty, with humble aport,
Bounty, riches, and womanly feature,
God better wot than my pen can report:
Wisdom, largess, estate, and cunning sure,
In every point so guided her measure,

In word, in deed, in shape, in countenance,
That nature might no more her child avance!

And when she walked had a little thraw
Under the sweete greene boughis bent,
Her fair fresh face, as white as any snaw,
She turned has, and furth her wayis went;
But then began mine aches and torment,
To see her part and follow I na might;
Methought the day was turned into night.

James I of Scotland (1394-1437)

Song of Fairies Robbing an Orchard

We, the Fairies, blithe and antic,
Of dimensions not gigantic,
Though the moonshine mostly keep us,
Oft in orchards frisk and peep us.

Stolen sweets are always sweeter,
Stolen kisses much completer,
Stolen looks are nice in chapels,
Stolen, stolen, be your apples.

When to bed the world are bobbing,
Then's the time for orchard-robbing;
Yet the fruit were scarce worth peeling,
Were it not for stealing, stealing.

Leigh Hunt (1784-1859)

The Seeds of Love

I sowed the seeds of love

To blossom all the spring,

In April, May, or else in June,

When the small birds do sing:

A gardener standing by,

I desired him to choose for me;

He picked out the lily, the violet, and pink,

But I refused all three.

The lily I refused,

Because it faded so soon;

The violet and pink I overlooked,

Resolved was to tarry till June:

In June the red roses bud,

Oh, that is a lover for me;

But I have often aimed at the red rose-bud,

And I have gained the willow tree.

The gardener standing by,

He prayed me to have a care,

For the thorn that grew on the red rose-bush,

A venomous thorn they were:

A venomous thorn indeed,

For still I feel the smart;
And every time I did it touch,
It pricked my tender heart.
Away you fading flowers,
No more I will you touch,
That all the world may plainly see
I loved one flower too much.

Mrs. Fleetwood Habergham (c. 17th century)

LINES: THE COLD EARTH SLEPT BELOW

The cold earth slept below;
Above the cold sky shone;
And all around,
With a chilling sound,
From caves of ice and fields of snow
The breath of night like death did flow
Beneath the sinking moon.

The wintry hedge was black;
The green grass was not seen;
The birds did rest
On the bare thorn's breast,
Whose roots, beside the pathway track,
Had bound their folds o'er many a crack
Which the frost had made between.

Thine eyes glow'd in the glare
Of the moon's dying light;
As a fen-fire's beam
On a sluggish stream

Gleams dimly – so the moon shone there,
And it yellow'd the strings of thy tangled hair,
That shook in the wind of night.

The moon made thy lips pale, beloved;
The wind made thy bosom chill;
The night did shed
On thy dear head
Its frozen dew, and thou didst lie
Where the bitter breath of the naked sky
Might visit thee at will.

Percy Bysshe Shelley (1792–1822)

Upon My Lady Carlisle's Walking in Hampton Court Garden

Dialogue

Thomas Carew. John Suckling.

Thom.

Didst thou not find the place inspired,
And flowers, as if they had desired
No other sun, start from their beds,
And for a sight steal out their heads?
Heardst thou not music when she talked?
And didst not find that as she walked
She threw rare perfumes all about,
Such as bean-blossoms newly out,
Or chafèd spices give? –

J.S.

I must confess those perfumes, Tom,
I did not smell; nor found that from

Her passing by ought sprung up new.
The flowers had all their birth from you;
For I passed o'er the self-same walk
And did not find one single stalk
Of anything that was to bring
This unknown after-after-spring.

Thom.

Dull and insensible, couldst see
A thing so near a deity
Move up and down, and feel no change?

J.S.

None, and so great, were alike strange;
I had my thoughts, but not your way.
All are not born, sir, to the bay.
Alas! Tom, I am flesh and blood,
And was consulting how I could
In spite of masks and hoods descry
The parts denied unto the eye.
I was undoing all she wore,

And had she walked but one turn more,
Eve in her first state had not been
More naked or more plainly seen.

Thom.

'Twas well for thee she left the place;
There is great danger in that face.
But hadst thou viewed her leg and thigh,
And upon that discovery
Searched after parts that are more dear
(As fancy seldom stops so near),
No time or age had ever seen
So lost a thing as thou hadst been.

Sir John Suckling (1609–1642)

Astrophil and Stella, Sonnet 82

Nymph of the garden where all beauties be,
Beauties which do in excellency pass
His who till death looked in a watery glass,
Or hers whom nak'd the Trojan boy did see;
Sweet garden-nymph, which keeps the cherry-tree
Whose fruit doth far the Hesperian taste surpass,
Most sweet-fair, most fair-sweet, do not, alas,
From coming near those cherries banish me.
For though, full of desire, empty of wit,
Admitted late by your best-gracèd grace,
I caught at one of them, and hungry bit,
Pardon that fault; once more grant me the place;
And I do swear, even by the same delight,
I will but kiss, I never more will bite.

Sir Philip Sidney (1554-1586)

THERE IS A GARDEN IN HER FACE

There is a garden in her face
Where roses and white lilies grow;
A heav'nly paradise is that place
Wherein all pleasant fruits do flow.
There cherries grow which none may buy,
Till "Cherry ripe" themselves do cry.

Those cherries fairly do enclose
Of orient pearl a double row,
Which when her lovely laughter shows,
They look like rose-buds fill'd with snow;
Yet them nor peer nor prince can buy,
Till "Cherry ripe" themselves do cry.

Her eyes like angels watch them still,
Her brows like bended bows do stand,
Threat'ning with piercing frowns to kill
All that attempt with eye or hand
Those sacred cherries to come nigh,
Till "Cherry ripe" themselves do cry.

Thomas Campion (1567-1620)

To the Garden, the World

To the garden, the world, anew ascending,
Potent mates, daughters, sons, preluding,
The love, the life of their bodies, meaning and being,
Curious, here behold my resurrection, after slumber;
The revolving cycles, in their wide sweep, having
brought me again,
Amorous, mature – all beautiful to me – all wondrous;
My limbs, and the quivering fire that ever plays through
them, for reasons, most wondrous;
Existing, I peer and penetrate still,
Content with the present – content with the past,
By my side, or back of me, Eve following,
Or in front, and I following her just the same.

Walt Whitman (1819-1892)

THE SICK ROSE

O rose, thou art sick!
The invisible worm,
That flies in the night,
In the howling storm,

Has found out thy bed
Of crimson joy,
And his dark secret love
Does thy life destroy.

William Blake (1757–1827)

Sonnet 94

They that have power to hurt and will do none,
That do not do the thing they most do show,
Who, moving others, are themselves as stone,
Unmoved, cold, and to temptation slow:
They rightly do inherit heaven's graces
And husband nature's riches from expense;
They are the lords and owners of their faces,
Others but stewards of their excellence.
The summer's flower is to the summer sweet
Though to itself it only live and die,
But if that flower with base infection meet,
The basest weed outbraves his dignity:
For sweetest things turn sourest by their deeds;
Lilies that fester smell far worse than weeds.

William Shakespeare (1564-1616)

Garden Scenes

Scenes

Portraits of Nature

Fringed Gentians

Near where I live there is a lake
As blue as blue can be, winds make
It dance as they go blowing by.
I think it curtseys to the sky.

It's just a lake of lovely flowers
And my Mamma says they are ours;
But they are not like those we grow
To be our very own, you know.

We have a splendid garden, there
Are lots of flowers everywhere;
Roses, and pinks, and four o'clocks
And hollyhocks, and evening stocks.

Mamma lets us pick them, but never
Must we pick any gentians – ever!
For if we carried them away
They'd die of homesickness that day.

Amy Lowell (1874-1925)

THE LITTLE GARDEN

A little garden on a bleak hillside
Where deep the heavy, dazzling mountain snow
Lies far into the spring. The sun's pale glow
Is scarcely able to melt patches wide
About the single rose bush. All denied
Of nature's tender ministries. But no, –
For wonder-working faith has made it blow
With flowers many hued and starry-eyed.
Here sleeps the sun long, idle summer hours;
Here butterflies and bees fare far to rove
Amid the crumpled leaves of poppy flowers;
Here four o'clocks, to the passionate night above
Fling whiffs of perfume, like pale incense showers.
A little garden, loved with a great love!

Amy Lowell (1874-1925)

THE BROKEN FOUNTAIN

Oblong, its jutted ends rounding into circles,
The old sunken basin lies with its flat, marble lip
An inch below the terrace tiles.
Over the stagnant water
Slide reflections:
The blue-green of coned yews;
The purple and red of trailing fuchsias
Dripping out of marble urns;
Bright squares of sky
Ribbed by the wake of a swimming beetle.
Through the blue-bronze water
Wavers the pale uncertainty of a shadow.
An arm flashes through the reflections,
A breast is outlined with leaves.
Outstretched in the quiet water
The statue of a Goddess slumbers.
But when Autumn comes
The beech leaves cover her with a golden counter-pane.

Amy Lowell (1874-1925)

A Brilliant Day

O keen pellucid air! nothing can lurk
Or disavow itself on this bright day;
The small rain-plashes shine from far away,
The tiny emmet glitters at his work;
The bee looks blithe and gay, and as she plies
Her task, and moves and sidles round the cup
Of this spring flower, to drink its honey up,
Her glassy wings, like oars that dip and rise,
Gleam momently. Pure-bosom'd, clear of fog,
The long lake glistens, while the glorious beam
Bespangles the wet joints and floating leaves
Of water-plants, whose every point receives
His light; and jellies of the spawning frog,
Unmark'd before, like piles of jewels seem!

Charles Turner (1808-1879)

Purple Clover

There is a flower that bees prefer,
And butterflies desire;
To gain the purple democrat
The humming-birds aspire.

And whatsoever insect pass,
A honey bears away
Proportioned to his several dearth
And her capacity.

Her face is rounder than the moon,
And ruddier than the gown
Of orchis in the pasture,
Or rhododendron worn.

She doth not wait for June;
Before the world is green
Her sturdy little countenance
Against the wind is seen,

Contending with the grass,
Near kinsman to herself,
For privilege of sod and sun,
Sweet litigants for life.

And when the hills are full,
And newer fashions blow,
Doth not retract a single spice
For pang of jealousy.

Her public is the noon,
Her providence the sun,
Her progress by the bee proclaimed
In sovereign, swerveless tune.

The bravest of the host,
Surrendering the last,
Nor even of defeat aware
When cancelled by the frost.

Emily Dickinson (1830-1886)

In the Garden

A bird came down the walk:
He did not know I saw;
He bit an angle-worm in halves
And ate the fellow, raw.

And then he drank a dew
From a convenient grass,
And then hopped sidewise to the wall
To let a beetle pass.

He glanced with rapid eyes
That hurried all abroad, –
They looked like frightened beads, I thought;
He stirred his velvet head

Like one in danger; cautious,
I offered him a crumb,
And he unrolled his feathers
And rowed him softer home

Than oars divide the ocean,
Too silver for a seam,
Or butterflies, off banks of noon,
Leap, plashless, as they swim.

Emily Dickinson (1830-1886)

A Garden in the Desert

So light and soft the days fall –
Like petals one by one
Down from yon tree whose flowers all
Must vanish in the sun.

Like almond-petals down, dear,
Odorous, rosy-white,
Falling to our green world here
Off the thick boughs of night.

One like another still lies –
Tomorrow is today.
Always the buzzing bee flies,
Who never flies away.

Ever the same blue sky rounds
Its chalice for the sun.
The mountains at the world's bounds
Their purple chorals run.

And ever you and I, friend,
Free of this mortal scheme,
Look out beyond desire's end
And dream the spacious dream.

Harriet Monroe (1860–1936)

THE AIR PLANT

Grand Cayman
This tuft that thrives on saline nothingness,
Inverted octopus with heavenward arms
Thrust parching from a palm-bole hard by the cove –
A bird almost – of almost bird alarms,

Is pulmonary to the wind that jars
Its tentacles, horrific in their lurch.
The lizard's throat, held bloated for a fly,
Balloons but warily from this throbbing perch.

The needles and hack-saws of cactus bleed
A milk of earth when stricken off the stalk;
But this, – defenseless, thornless, sheds no blood,
Almost no shadow but – the air's thin talk.

Angelic Dynamo! Ventriloquist of the Blue!
While beachward creeps the shark-swept Spanish Main
By what conjunctions do the winds appoint
Its apotheosis, at last – the hurricane!

Hart Crane (1899-1932)

TALL AMBROSIA

Among the signs of autumn I perceive
The Roman wormwood (called by learned men
Ambrosia elatior, food for gods, –
For to impartial science the humblest weed
Is as immortal once as the proudest flower –)
Sprinkles its yellow dust over my shoes
As I cross the now neglected garden.
 – We trample under foot the food of gods
And spill their nectar in each drop of dew –
My honest shoes, fast friends that never stray
Far from my couch, thus powdered, countryfied,
Bearing many a mile the marks of their adventure,
At the post-house disgrace the Gallic gloss
Of those well dressed ones who no morning dew
Nor Roman wormwood ever have been through,
Who never walk but are *transported* rather –
For what old crime of theirs I do not gather.

Henry David Thoreau (1817-1862)

THE WORM

When the earth is turned in spring
The worms are fat as anything.

And birds come flying all around
To eat the worms right off the ground.

They like worms just as much as I
Like bread and milk and apple pie.

And once, when I was very young,
I put a worm right on my tongue.

I didn't like the taste a bit,
And so I didn't swallow it.

But oh, it makes my Mother squirm
Because she *thinks* I ate that worm!

Ralph Bergengren (1871-1947)

INDEX